IF I CHANGE, SO CAN THE WRLD

PAULA PLUCK

Forty Positive Steps to Global Togetherness

POLAIR PUBLISHING · LONDON

With illustrations by Villamor Cruz and Bodel Rikys
First published October 2005

British Library Cataloguing-in-Publication Data
A catalogue record for this book is available
from the British Library
ISBN 1-905398-06-9

Acknowledgments

Loving thanks to Colum Hayward for believing in me as a writer and making this book possible. Your advice and encouragement have been a great inspiration to me. To Villamor Cruz and Bodel Rikys, who bring to life the ideas in this book with fabulous illustrations that make my heart smile. Your talents combine beautifully and I am extremely grateful to you both. For my mum, thank you for always reminding me 'she who dares wins'. You are amazing. Your limitless love and giving fill my heart with love. You are a gift to all who know you. My gorgeous husband Mark, who has patiently challenged me to write simple, practical and easily understood concepts in the creation of this work. Your friendship and willingness to support me is truly beautiful. Love you. My beautiful boys Ben and Dan, I love you. You compel me to create the loveliest version of living for us all. You are gorgeous. You give me the happiest heart and I am sure your shining beauty always will.

Disclaimer

This book gives non-specific, general advice and should not be relied on as a substitute for proper medical consultations. The author and publisher cannot accept responsibility for illness arising out of failure to seek medical advice where appropriate.

Set in Copperplate Gothic and Century Gothic at the Publisher
and Printed in Great Britain by
Cambridge University Press

CONTENTS

World Change

SECTION 1: DESIGN FOR A BETTER LIFE

AUTHOR'S PREFACE

IN THIS BOOK I share how I reconnected to the gentleness and love of my intuitive self, and how that experience blossomed into a sense of oneness with the world around me. In short, personal love leads to the greater love of 'becoming part of the growing community for positive loving development on a global scale'.

It all started one day when in complete exhaustion I asked myself, 'How did I get here?' I was trapped in the revolving doors of stress. Emotionally, mentally and physically drained. On the surface it all looked great. I had the ideal: adorable children, loving partner, successful career, wonderful sex, holidays and a beautiful home.

If my outer world looked so great, what was making me feel so bad, I mused? Aside from being in the grip of appalling and constant sleep-deprivation, increasingly experiencing moments of self-panic and ruminating on the eternal question, 'Am I good enough?', I felt a prisoner of war in my own body.

Let's not pretend that however successfully we do it, juggling family, relationships, career and the ordinary pressures of life is always easy. It isn't. Life's changes can be a constant challenge. Add,

This journey is made up of forty steps ... symbolic of the number of weeks it takes to give birth to the miracle of a new life.

in my case, giving birth to twins; bereavement (my father), and all the stresses of relocation in just over a year, you can see why the intensity of change might have begun to feel unbearable!

Feeling dissatisfied and stressed out, I longed to balance the frustrations and hopes of my mind and emotions. One thing was for sure, I'd read enough 'gurus' to know we get what we focus on. Also my career had centred around offering a practical approach to change management in the workplace, to promote personal and organisational development.

I decided it was time to create change that supported *me*.

You are about to read the results! In this book I share the steps I took to empower myself and create a path of personal liberation. I share how I evaluated my thinking and feelings to redesign my life and make space for the person I wanted to be and the life I wanted to live.

The steps ask you bravely to root out negativity in your heart and make way for the loveliest version of yourself. They ask you to connect to your divinity and by extending your loving awareness across the world to develop a sense of global citizenship.

I feel certain the cumulative effect of our thoughts, words and actions will ultimately change the world. I have always been inspired by the thought that we individually have the power to make the world a better place to live in, by the way we think, act and speak.

*

I am aware you could quite easily read through this book in an hour or two. However to work with the practices will take a little longer. It is a good idea to take small steps in changing yourself. Try starting with thoughts and habits, which are quite easy to change, to build a sense of confidence in the process.

It is also very helpful to keep a journal. You can record how you have felt moving through the steps. For example: how do you feel about the steps as you take them? Have others noticed a change in you? On which steps did you encounter the most emotional and mental resistance? How are you experiencing the change?

The most important thing is to learn as much as possible in the change process. Lastly, as with everything, you'll get out of the practices just what you put into them!

This journey is made up of forty steps. Symbolic of the number of weeks it takes to give birth to the miracle of a new life. Thank you for joining me. Enjoy the challenges of recreating yourself, become truly happy with the 'design of your life' and know you can inspire world change with your actions today.

Paula Pluck
Isle of Man
September 2005

BUDDHA SAID, 'Look within, you are the Buddha'. I remember reading that statement and thinking 'Am I *really* a Buddha in waiting?' (this is how some Buddhists see us). This was exciting. Imagine the seeds of pure liberated love are within us all, just waiting to grow. Isn't that an amazing thought? What if from birth we as a society expected all children to develop into bright, wonderful, loving, peaceful, happy, joyous, liberated individuals?

Wouldn't the world be a better place? The possibilities for humanity would be limitless. This shift in thinking would steadily create a whole new world where love, peace, joy, compassion and kindness are the norm and death from poverty, hate, abuse, war, murder or starvation cease to exist.

I had to ask myself 'Does my thinking support the type of growth and ideal I want for our children as described above?' The answer was NO! I began to see I was weakening myself with unsupportive internal dialogue, which at best kept me surviving and at worst left me frustrated, dissatisfied, unfulfilled, and the like. I had long believed that my thoughts were creating my life, yet unbelievably I hadn't really ever taken the time out to ensure they were creating the life I wanted!

I started to recognize that the very simple idea, that world peace is connected to individual personal peace, was really true!

At first this confused me. Naturally, I realized cheerful loving behaviour lifted other people's emotions. On the other hand, I didn't like the idea of my consciousness being connected to the consciousness of people who act in the most gruesome ways.

Then I started looking at human nature as having two very distinct levels of experience. The first is our personalities joining together to contribute to the energy that makes up our world. Whether we are the sinner or the saint, we are joined by the energy we create collectively.

The second part of our nature I believe is divine. Our divinity, which is a true and beautiful expression of love, is encased in the physical body. For me it is our expression of the eternal Source, the one we call God. I started to really see that the simplicity of life is wrapped beautifully in the law of love and that only by accepting the unity of all life could we bring freedom to individual and world consciousness.

Choosing to see these two levels of experience and accept them reinforces an understanding that we are all within each other, connected eternally by our spirit and physically by our collective choice. The concepts and practices in this book try to embrace ways of harmonizing our physical and divine nature to forge positive, bright and beautiful change in our personal life and the world we live in.

The idea is that we cannot condemn war or suffering if we ourselves are filled with conflict, whether our pain is obvious or subtly hidden. In this light, where the grief of personal, national and international wars once reigned, freedom can flourish. Our own release brings true freedom of choice, a willingness to walk a path of common humanity and connection with the rest of life in all we say, think and do.

WE ARE RESPONSIBLE! The fabulous thing about happiness is that it's a question of the way we think, what we tell ourselves, how we care for ourselves, and how we contribute to the world around us.

We may be very determined, sometimes aggressive, stressed, competitive, critical, impatient, fear-thinking people, where our happiness is dependent on striving for more—a better house, car, job, friends, wealth, etc. Or we may see ourselves as more 'heart' people, working for tenderness, compassion, unity, intuition and joy in our lives. This type of happiness is not reliant on what we've got, but more on 'who' we are. In honesty, we'll sometimes be a mix of them both.

Why not consider the motivation behind your thinking? Are your thoughts fear-driven? Take an example. Maybe you think other people are responsible for your happiness; or you give yourself a hard time for not getting it right. Do you think one person can't make a difference to the world? Are you too busy to slow down? Or do you worry there is not enough, money, love, whatever...?

Do you need to change your thinking so as to be more loving and supportive? This could be done by acknowledging you are responsible for your happiness; believing you are worthy, as is your opinion; trusting in life and knowing you are supported; accepting sometimes you make mistakes; slowing down if you are anxious or stressed and most of all by knowing you can make a difference to the world.

The first thing I did on my own journey was to listen to my heart and find out more about myself. Try this out for *yourself.* Take a piece of paper and head it

'WHO AM I?'

Write down everything that comes to mind. All kinds of ideas will come to you, both good and bad, positive and negative. Just list them all.

Now review your answers to the question. Ask yourself, 'Am I happy with ... the person I think I am?'

How can you create a more beautiful version of your self? Model the great teachers and philosophers. They all share, in one way or another, that when we know ourself we know heaven. *As Jesus said 'Where your treasure is, there will your heart be also.'*

SECTION ONE   **DESIGN FOR A BETTER LIFE**

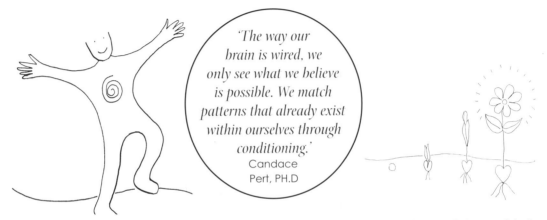

'The way our brain is wired, we only see what we believe is possible. We match patterns that already exist within ourselves through conditioning.'
Candace
Pert, PH.D

THE NEXT THING I DID was to create a personal vision clearly stating where I was going and where I wanted to be at the end of my life.

To help with this, I asked myself

'WHO DO I THINK I WANT TO BE?'

Do the same. Write down everything that comes to mind. Ignore doubts and let yourself be ambitious, entrepreneurial and true to your heart. Include what makes you happy. Don't underestimate yourself. You *are a seed of pure potential—ready to grow into the loveliest version of yourself.*

Take real responsibility for yourself. Dedicate yourself to breaking free from old patterns that limit you. Let go of everything that stops you being as wonderful as you can be.

Now imagine what you could be doing more of? List three things that make you really happy. Really work toward creating the life you want.

I LOVE THE FACT that we have the power within us to transform our lives by the way we think, act and speak. For me, recognizing my inner strength to create personal change is a major part of the journey to happiness. I had to release so many thoughts and feelings which had stopped me embracing the joy of living. Most importantly, I had to believe in my ability to create the change I wanted to see in my life. I started this process off by

❂   remembering some of the things I have achieved in life. Why not list three of your achievements now?

❂   accepting that the above list proves I have the ability to achieve my desires, as do you.

❂   listing at least three things I really wanted to achieve in life. Please do this also.

And lastly

❂   every time I had a negative thought about myself I turned it around into a positive one. With practice, this gets easier.

As we move through the steps there will be opportunities to expand on your goals and desires. For now the most important thing is that you really believe you can achieve contentment and satisfaction in your life through your chosen design. Invest your thoughts in the idea that you are completely worthy of all of your dreams.

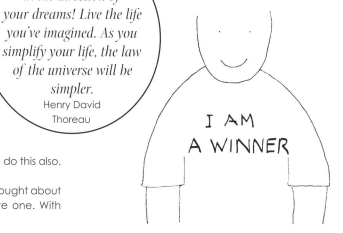

> *Go confidently in the direction of your dreams! Live the life you've imagined. As you simplify your life, the law of the universe will be simpler.*
> Henry David Thoreau

I AM A WINNER

TO GROW AND TRANSFORM our life into what its truest potential allows, we must learn to work with our energy to support our highest good. Energy is wonderfully dynamic—and it changes all the time, depending on our thoughts, feelings and actions. Take a moment to consider this idea: 'We can influence and be influenced by the energy around us'.

Each person has a unique energy field, sometimes referred to as the Aura. Our aura interacts with the energies of others, as well as those of plants and animals. In a very obvious sense, we are aware of this all time. You know the type of thing. 'When he walked into the room you could cut the air with a knife'; or, 'The joy in that person lifts your mood immediately.' 'The animal could sense your fear....'

Having said that, it is easy to see that we can choose to enhance our energy by surrounding ourselves with people who raise our energy levels, who see the best in us and want the best for us. Or conversely, we can surround ourselves with people who seem addicted to negativity and quite literally drain our energy. 'To create positive world change we first must create positive personal change.'

'To create positive world change we first must create positive personal change.'

As our thoughts create energy, it becomes clear that we can add to the blocked energy in our bodies, or alternatively add to freeflowing, joyous energy in our bodies. We can evolve and transform our individual energy-system so it in turn increases the creation of beauty and love in our worlds energy system. We may not hold the whole world in our hands, but we hold our part of it!

The fantastic thing about energy is we can take control of it, and create in our energy field a greater sense of happiness and calm. We can use our understanding of energy to handle stress or enhance our ability to manage change.

The magical mix of our energy field is more than our thoughts. It is our state of being, made up of our emotional, mental, physical and spiritual perception. The world around us mirrors our inner thinking and feelings. By giving ourselves the gift of joy and appreciation we will find joy and appreciation in our world.

WE CAN MEASURE if changing our thoughts will truly make our life better. How? By living our life to our chosen potential, by our chosen design. Try out the thinking ideas on this page. Make your own decisions: don't depend on my thoughts, but test your own and see if changing your thinking really does make you happier.

If the home of your thinking needs a good cleanse from negative or painful thinking, the challenge of change will require discipline. Once we start monitoring our thoughts, we might not like to share just how many of them are repetitive, negative, critical or maybe even spiteful or mean.

I worked with the ideas and questions opposite in order to confront and change my thinking. They help you recognize if your internal chatter is positive and supportive or negative and unsupportive.

'Whatsoever things are true, whatsoever things are honest, whatsoever things are just, whatsoever things are pure, whatsoever things are lovely, whatsoever things are of good report; if there be any virtue, and if there be any praise, think on these things.'
St Paul

THINKING ABOUT HOW YOU THINK

✪ Pretend everyone can hear every thought you have for a week. As the week goes by, are you pleased with or embarrassed by your thoughts?

✪ See if you can go a whole day without judging or criticizing anyone. You'll feel happier—and you'll definitely begin the process of controlling your thoughts so that they don't control you.

✪ Consider how you can change your thinking to support the world we live in.

✪ Lastly, list two or three things you can change about the way you think:
   a) to make your life happier and
   b) to make the world a better place to live in.

YOU, LIKE EVERY HUMAN BEING, ARE A MARVELLOUS CREATION. So clever are we that we actually create our world, not only with our conscious thoughts, but also our unconscious thinking. The latter includes instinctive things we are born with, such as breathing and digestion, as well as learning we acquire, like walking and talking. Our subconscious thoughts are a collection of our repeated conscious thoughts and inner knowledge.

We are what we think; all that we are arises with our thoughts. With our thoughts, we make our world.
Buddha

Not all of our thoughts and feelings are ones we want to have. Imagine you occasionally spilled drinks as a child and your dad repeatedly said you were clumsy? Well, you are likely to have believed him and to have conscious thoughts and feelings associated with that. The more a conscious thought is repeated, the stronger the subconscious belief becomes.

Recognizing these patterns and taking responsibilty for our thoughts is very liberating. It enables us to design the future of our choice. We have a personal responsibility to protect ourselves from negative, unsupportive thinking. Instead, we can move from painful to beautiful, limited to limitless thinking now. It is our choice.

Step 6 continues to challenge our conditioning by going deeper into our early learning. Take a piece of paper and write down three supportive and three unsupportive things you have learnt about yourself while growing up, from:
❂ *Parents;*
❂ *Teachers;*
❂ *Friends;*
❂ *Authority figures in the community.*

From this exercise you'll be able to identify negative patterns, ones that don't support you. Please don't be tempted to get stuck in the pain of your negative conditioning. Try to accept you can't change the past, but you can stop your out-of-date thinking or someone else's limited vision guiding your future!

WHEN YOUR DEFENCES ARE FLIMSY and you're feeling out of sorts, this technique is a gorgeous lift. As they say, 'Smile and the whole world smiles with you…' Try this, for a smile. I have developed it from the beautiful and powerful healing meditation the Inner Smile by Mantak Chia.

To begin, sit quietly and just allow your thoughts to settle and yourself to become calm. Let your breathing guide you into a sense of calm. As you inhale, sense yourself smiling. As you exhale sense this beautiful smile filling your whole body with warmth, happiness and peace. Now, breathing in, smile into your heart; and breathing out, feel calm in your heart.

Now sense the warmth of your smile at the corners of your mouth. Gently raise the corners of your mouth a little further and enjoy the lovely, increased sensation of your smile. Become aware of the happier energy your smile creates within you….

> *The Taoists taught that a constant inner smile, a smile to oneself, insured health, happiness and longevity. Why? Smiling to yourself is like basking in love: you become your own best friend. Living with an inner smile is to live in harmony with yourself.*
> Mantak Chia

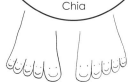

Focus your attention on the warmth of your smile around your eyes. Now gently raise the corners of your eyes too, until you experience a lovely sense of happiness smiling behind your eyes also. Now sense the corners of your eyes and mouth connecting, giving a deeper sense of warmth, and happiness within you. 'All you've got to do is smile.' After five minutes or so of this lovely practice your original anxiety will appear less daunting, leaving you to share in the eastern wisdom: *'This too shall pass.'*

Before finishing, imagine your toes smiling at you. The madness of it all will unleash a greater smile inside you, which you can imagine flowing right up the whole of your body like a cosy warm rush of love, filling you with easy 'can do', 'it's okay' feelings.

WHEN THE PRESSURE GETS TOO MUCH, then like many north-of-England women my mum repeats the wonderful saying 'Stop the world, I want to get off.' I think we can all feel like this at times, and while we can't exactly stop the world, we can look at ways of slowing our personal world down.

The tried and tested way of inviting peace and calm into our lives is meditation. Anyone can meditate. It is not reserved for the mystical elite, it is a natural and beautiful way to help you feel less anxious and more in control. Meditation promotes clarity and calm. It increases happiness and wellbeing, but is at the same time an accepted tonic and energizer. It is a brilliant way to recharge our batteries.

There are a number of meditation exercises in this book. If you can practise them with friends, taking turns to read through the meditations that will be great. If not, you may like to record them. Remember to find a quiet time where you will be undisturbed, and to wear comfortable clothing.

PAUSING FOR PEACE

Light a candle, as an object of focus, to aid this meditation. Gently let your gaze rest on the candle, and continue for a couple of minutes. The still golden flame may fill you with a sense of calm and warmth. As you gaze, you become aware of a sense of spaciousness around the candle and within yourself.

Now close your eyes and imagine the light of the candle being a light of peace. Invite peace into your whole being, silently affirming, 'I am peace....' See this peace flowing through your whole body, as a golden light.... Use the breath to guide the inflow of peace. On the outbreath, let go of the busy chatter of your mind....

After a minute or two, during which you continue to let the inbreath guide the inflow of peace, see and feel the warmth and comfort of golden light flooding your whole body with radiance and peace. Enjoy this simple relaxed state for ten or twenty minutes, before gently returning your awareness to the room.

A SIMPLE BREATHING FOCUS

Sit in a comfortable position with your back straight to help you achieve a sense of poise and alertness. This also helps you breathe well and prevents the mind from becoming sleepy.

Now simply turn your attention to your breathing. Breathe naturally, preferably through the nostrils, without attempting to control your breath.

Let yourself become aware of the sensation of the breath as it enters and leaves the nostrils. This breathing sensation acts as our focus to relax. It is useful to get into the habit of letting the breath guide you into deeper relaxation wherever possible. Try this practice next time you're in a traffic jam!

If you find your mind has wandered off, following your thoughts, just return your focus to the breath. After a few minutes practising this breathing exercise, you can move on to your chosen meditation.

WHETHER IT IS DEALING with a boardroom presentation or three-year old, twin boys devilishly smearing jam over the new kitchen blinds, meditation helps! Was it Gandhi, amid his campaign to create a free and self-governing India, who is reported to have said, 'I have so much to do today, I will need to meditate twice as long'?

Meditation really does make it easier to respond positively to challenging situations in our daily lives. It helps us become centered. You'll find a personal story about this over the page. When we lose our centre, we say and do things we don't mean; we make mistakes, we project internal conflict onto the world, and we lose our peace.

In meditation, we let go of our conscious thoughts, opening the way for us to tap into the reservoir of inner strength inside ourselves.

To calm down the senses, a gentle relaxation technique is always a good preamble to meditation, and something involving the breath is even better. Try the simple breathing technique on the left before you move on to the next meditation in this book. It will help you in any meditations you might want to do.

My First Dance with Infinite Consciousness

This all happened about eleven years ago. I was feeling bullied by my boss and desperately upset by her. I won't bore you with the details: suffice it to say that she seemed at the time to be the most monstrous individual I'd ever had the misfortune of meeting. I was so cross with her I thought I might explode!

I thought about ringing my friends and drinking copious amounts of wine, and then something in me thought, 'No: this feels awful, don't mask it with alcohol'. Exhausted with anger, frustration and injustice I went home. I prepared a candlelit bath, with tranquil music and lavender essence, to calm me down, before setting about meditating.

I like to use the breath, visualization and prayer in meditation. I simply breathe a little deeper, sensing I am filling my heart with golden loving light, before praying. On this particular day, in a flash I found myself caught up in the brightest white light. My mind became totally clear and I was filled with a beautiful sense of completeness. In this state my troubles just ceased to exist, for that time.

But more than that had happened in that flash. I had glimpsed the consciousness of avatars. Amazingly I could only feel love for my boss, as I recognized we were connected at our source, each struggling along from our own particular level of consciousness in our daily living. It was so beautiful, so blissful, that only thoughts of love and joy could emanate from this level of consciousness.

Astonishingly I'd had my first *nirvana* experience in my flat, alone, inside myself! As Jesus shared, 'The kingdom of heaven is within you'. Truly. The individual story I'd being telling myself about my life, all of a sudden became potent with possibilities. My feeling of interconnectedness with everyone and everything was breathtaking.

The power and peace of meditation can perform miracles, even if they are not as astounding as walking on water. More simply, our perception changes, and we gain a sense of personal power, to deal with our life-circumstances—even the more frustrating ones!

WE'RE NOW AT THE REALLY EXCITING MOMENT. For the minute we understand that our thoughts are creating our reality, it can be a moment of brilliance in our life! Why? Because we are absolutely ready for the shift, the change in thinking designed to make our life happier and more fulfilled. With our new thinking, we enter a world of infinite possibilities, where the science of consciousness becomes our own individual experiment.

Pretend you are a writer. Imagine what would be in your new script, entitled 'A wonderful life'. Consider the commentary, think of all the lovely things contained in a wonderful life.

Consider how you would feel if it all came true. Feel your posture change as you do so. Notice the words you use in your account and the dialogue you use to express this.

Now ask yourself:

a) 'How can I change my thinking to achieve this?'

b) 'What can I do now to begin creating a more beautiful reality in my life today!'

SECTION 2: COURAGE ON THE CATWALK OF LIFE

IT TAKES COURAGE TO CLEAN UP OUR PLANET, especially when you realize the starting point is you! We are linked by energy, and our individual response to mental and emotional stress influences the world around us. Our thoughts and feelings affect collective consciousness, which clearly impacts on how things play out, not only for our own lives but for the planet too.

Yes, we all have a personal responsibility to create a better world. But don't see it as a burden! Think of it as a remarkable opportunity to join in the creation of a beautiful world. Just by doing what we can to promote greater happiness and love in ourselves, we shall naturally move closer to the ultimate aim, of making the world a better place to live in.

Our inner world is not just a world of thought, it is a world of feeling; and our emotional life can be affected by the world around us, sometimes eliciting responses we do not want or expect. Here we find ourselves responding to old emotional programming we thought we had resolved.

Make room for the beautiful shining self to emerge from within!

It is really frustrating when we feel nervous, angry, or hurt when we don't want to, isn't it? This happens because although we've changed our basic thinking, our emotions still instinctively react to the old stimulus. Whether it is stress or joy, love or hate, the power of our emotions plays a key role in our sense of happiness.

Every one of us can have reasons for self-horror. We may have or remember thoughts of violence towards someone who has hurt us. Or we may experience inappropriate lust or desire that would result in hurting another person. Whatever the emotions, we can use self-love and forgiveness as tools for letting go.

To bring harmony to difficult emotions we have to admit they exist, accept them and learn from them. We can't change things we don't understand or deny. Through contemplation and cultivating our self-confidence and sense of self-worth, we can release old pain and make room for the beautiful shining self to emerge from within.

DECIDING TO NURTURE OUR SPIRIT does not mean we need to hug trees or sit at the breakfast table in full lotus! It really means making an intelligent choice to support our body, mind and spirit. A few achievable lifestyle changes can contribute to the wellbeing and happiness not only of ourselves but our families, friends and even the planet.

A hectic lifestyle can really pollute us, leaving us feeling dense and heavy. Whether it is breathing contaminated air, living and working in artificial conditions, experiencing emotional and mental *angst*, filling the body with chemicals, or just plain old unconsciousness in our approach to living, life can become a toxic minefield.

We can combat these things and choose gentle, cleansing behaviours and ways of thinking to promote the flow of loving energy in and around our body, protecting us from the toxicity while keeping us energized and vibrant with life.

A few days of working on building our inner power by using ideas like those proposed in the next step can produce fabulous results! They include feeling intuitive, creative, peaceful, happy, physically strong, and being more radiant in appearance. Choosing to nurture our inner spirit also strengthens our resolve, giving us the courage to deal with the most trying circumstances in life, such as illness, the break-up of a relationship, a job loss or a bereavement.

When I work on clearing my inner clutter, I create rituals to cleanse the personal space around me too! For example a deep spring clean can represent the release of emotional pain. Or lighting a candle in my meditation space can become a cleansing light promoting health and harmony in my mind, body and spirit.

Whatever we do to make our life more beautiful and clear—no matter how minutely—it affects the rest of the world. Every step we take to increase the love in and around us is also a step to increasing the love in and around the world!

> 'We've been conditioned to believe that the external world is more real than the internal world. The new model of science says just the opposite. It says what's happening within us will create what's happening outside of us.'
> Dr Joseph Dispenza

CREATING THE LIFE OF OUR DREAMS calls for consistent, positive changes in the way we think, act and speak. Change can be obstructed by old patterns and damning conclusions we have made about life. Take a look at the following lists and ask yourself **'Do I increase my personal power by choosing a path that brings me more love, contentment, unity and joy, by the way I think act and speak?'**

Increasing Personal Power	Decreasing Personal Power
Laughter	Tension
Deep sleep	Disturbed sleeping patterns
Positive thinking	Negative thinking
Goals and purpose	Lack of direction
Sunshine	Staying indoors
Meditation & prayer	Boredom and worry
Deep Breathing	Shallow breathing
Fruits, vegetables & salad	Animal foods
Releasing blocked energy	Holding onto old resentments and pains
Fresh mineral water	Impure water
Relaxation therapy	Cigarettes, alcohol, refined sugar, coffee
Fresh Air	Conditioned air in offices or home
Natural remedies	Some drugs and vaccines
Exercise	Lack of physical activity

To integrate this step into your life get into the great habit of asking, **'Will this behaviour honour my dreams for living? Will it make me truly happy?'**

SECTION TWO   COURAGE ON THE CATWALK OF LIFE

LET'S NOT PRETEND THAT REDUCING CRAVINGS or releasing pain is easy. It takes determination and strong willpower. With this in mind, it is important to be gentle and loving with our self. See Step 21 for a lovely practice to support positive growth.

Changing our emotional responses is achievable, when we evaluate them. Even a slight change enables us to reflect on the disadvantages and advantages of having those responses—for instance, if we give way to anger, then peace eludes us. Or if we are too afraid to follow our dreams, we become unfulfilled. Remember you are the creator of your future not the victim of your past.

'Addiction is always a path of awakening'
Emmanuel

People can drink in exccess or take drugs because they believe it is their only route to happiness. Beliefs like this make cravings particularly hard to release. Whether a person is attached to drugs or alcohol, sex or success, if that attachment becomes painful, they need to ask, 'Why am I doing this to myself?'.

SOME IDEAS FOR REDUCING HARMFUL CRAVINGS AND RELEASING PAINFUL CONDITIONS

○ Developing an understanding of the damaging effects of the craving or pain you nurture.
○ Daily reminding yourself of the above to gradually help weaken your desire or attachment.
○ Asking yourself: 'Why am I prepared to harm myself with this habit or desire?' 'What inner pain am I hiding?'. And dealing with it, knowing you can turn to any outside help you may need to avoid dependence.
○ In the early stages, avoiding situations where you may be exposed to the object or people who will promote your unwanted cravings.
○ Replacing your desire or pain with a healthier option.
○ Adopting a positive attitude. Be patient and loving with yourself.
○ Rewarding yourself for recognizing your inner power to let go.

WE ALL HAVE A BEAUTIFUL INNER POWER and each of us can create our life by our chosen design. The better we feel about ourselves, the more relaxed and happy we feel, and the easier it is for us to be more gentle and loving in our response to life. Often we can feel trapped by how we see the world and people in it.

I now see people who hit a raw nerve in me as my greatest teacher, or as an indicator for healing. They give me the opportunity to alter the course of my future, standing as a signpost at a crossroads with the choice of 'Self love' or 'Self denial'.

'When we change our deepest beliefs and feelings about the world, our life and the planet can change too.'

I recognize that if I feel hurt or bad about myself as a result of someone's behaviour, it is because at some level I am buying into what they are saying. When someone elicits feelings which support old beliefs such as 'We are stupid/incapable/ unworthy/selfish/harsh/weak/dishonest' (delete whichever is not applicable!), I think it is because we have not cleansed the emotional energy in us that is linked to what they are saying.

So while our thinking is changing, we can still get the same emotional pull in situations, and so trigger the old emotional patterns that are both projected onto us, and created by us, in life. When we change our deepest beliefs and feelings about the world, our life and the planet can change too.

SECTION TWO   COURAGE ON THE CATWALK OF LIFE

LETTING GO OF PAIN AND FINDING FORGIVENESS can be tough, but the rewards of release are well worth it. We can hide our pain or fear so well within our consciousness, judging our emotions as bad or weak, ignoring, inflaming, denying or defensively masking them. When we think of old painful or harmful emotions, it is important to accept them and know we have the power to change them.

I practise the philosophy shared in the White Eagle Lodge's teachings. 'The Lodge', as it's affectionately known, uses the symbol of a six-pointed Star to represent perfect balance between our physical and divine nature. The upward-pointing triangle symbolises 'us' in our physical nature aspiring to divine love, and the downward triangle symbolises 'heavenly light' that can flood our whole being with love, wisdom and power. There's a picture of a three-dimensional Star on the next page that may be a perfect focus for your meditation.

When I am experiencing difficulty with letting go or surrendering to the conditions of my life, I visualize the Star filled with glorious blazing golden light and I feel that light filling my whole being with comfort and reassurance. It is so lovely to imagine this Starlight changing old negative feelings with love and healing.

> Try this simple meditation. Close your eyes. Breathing in, become aware of a Star filled with radiant light; and when breathing out, flood your whole being with this beautiful shining light. Now remaining dissociated, let the events of your life emerge before you.
>
> As each event emerges, whatever emotions it may hold for you, good or bad, flood it with vibrant powerful healing Starlight and let yourself release any old pain. You can direct your release further by affirming 'I am divine courage' or 'love' or 'peace'.
>
> Practising this can feel like a mental and physical sigh of relief, as it literally does lighten the load of tension, which has been building up in our body. It also promotes a lovely sensation of balance and peace.

*For more info visit **www.thestarlink.net.***

A FOCUS FOR MEDITATION

I Didn't Want you to Die

When my sister Michelle was diagnosed with leukaemia at the age of twenty-seven, I thought: 'It can't be true. It can't be happening to Shelly. Why was her life being interrupted so prematurely?' My normal little irritations lost their potency, and all of my anguish was for her.

Within weeks of her diagnosis, we were robbed of the temporary defense of denial, as her condition worsened fast. It was so hateful. Michelle's unexpected and serious illness rocked our world. The leukaemia relentlessly marched through her body, invading her life-force with a growing army of twenty-three million leukaemic cells a second. It was unbearable.

Michelle's treatment was in Liverpool. I moved there to be close to her, spending most of each day in the hospital. I didn't really understand death or dying; I just hoped she would get well. One day, she began talking to me about the reality of her situation. 'What if she died? What about her daughter, her husband, her dreams?'

As her fears and disappointments crowded in, she suddenly became really quiet and said, 'Why me?'. My heart was aching. It was inconceivable that my beautiful, gentle sister was being called upon to face death.

She then looked directly into my eyes and said, 'Why *not* me, though?'. For those moments her fear left her and a sense of acceptance seem to pour through her. I had such love for her, she was so brave and strong as she accepted her fear. I shall never forget the look of peace she had at that moment.

When she died, it was the most horrible feeling in the world. I remember sobbing on my knees. I didn't want her to die. I was bitter and angry for the loss of my sister. Torrents of great pain washed through my heart with the deepest anguish. Now, I know her spirit still lives on. As the lovely teachings of White Eagle share, 'In love there is no separation'. I feel her in my heart, and I know her presence in my heart is true.

Even though I know this, I sometimes still miss her and what might have been. In honour of her I share the following quotation, the source of which is unknown to me.

'Courage, sacrifice, determination, commitment, toughness, heart, talent, guts. That's what little girls are made of; to hell with sugar and spice!'

IT IS IMPORTANT TO BRING BALANCE INTO OUR LIVES. We have all had painful and joyous experiences in our time. Try not to lose sight of all the wonderful experiences in your life when working on healing your past. Celebrate the strengths you have created out of adversity, recognizing your fabulous courage and determination.

Yes, there are likely to be situations where we can forgive, and also situations where we have caused pain or harm to someone by hurting their feelings. To balance these situations, it is important to forgive those who have hurt us or to make amends with those we have hurt.

Think about the negative and positive effects of your emotions. How harmful are your unwanted feelings? How has your suffering made you the person you are today? Build on appreciating the distinctive ways you can help bring harmony to the energy of the world.

If we find it difficult to deal with some of our emotions, it can really help to chat with friends. A memory that has been locked away in the vault of our mind, when released, may come as a painful shock. If the shock is a powerful one, it may be important to seek professional support from a counsellor or therapist.

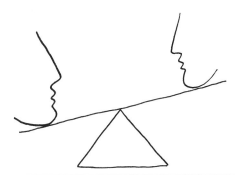

SECTION TWO   COURAGE ON THE CATWALK OF LIFE

IT IS IMPORTANT WE STAY IN TUNE with our inner thoughts and feelings. Sometimes people hear this but wonder how you do it. I use the technique of breath-awareness. It helps me increase my sense not just of what is going on around me, but also of my inner world too. It creates a sense of distance from the pull of our thoughts and emotions, giving us the opportunity to view ourself in a calmer state of mind.

In this heightened state of tranquillity, we can be more loving when choosing our responses, and that in turn can create more gentleness and love in our lives. With the pace of society continuing to accelerate, relaxation skills such as this are fast becoming the commonsense alternative to tension, stress, and anxiety. By creating just ten free minutes a day to practise breath-awareness, we can greatly reduce stress, anxiety and fear; improve insomnia, lessen depression, decrease blood pressure and reduce the risks of heart-related problems. To promote awareness, harmony and stillness, the following simple breathing exercise is great.

For a full guide to good breathing see DON'T HOLD YOUR BREATH by Jenny Beeken, in the same series as this book (ISBN 0-9545389-9-4).

BREATH AWARENESS

Sit quietly in a comfortable position and close your eyes. Start by breathing slowly, preferably through the nose, while mentally counting to five. As you inhale, sense and picture the air going down into your belly, rather than just your lungs. Rest your hands gently below your diaphragm and feel the belly expanding.

On the outbreath, feel the air completely emptying again for a count of five. You may feel the diaphragm pulling right in as you expel your breath. Do this ten to fifteen times during practice.

At all stages, really be aware of your breath. Feel it coming in and out through the nostrils or mouth. Imagine the clean air you take in being carried into your bloodstream and revitalizing it. Similarly, follow the air out in your mind; carry it right out of the body and discard it.

Use this diaphragmatic breathing during periods of anxiety or fear to release the symptoms of stress. If you are doing it properly, your shoulders and chest will have very little movement in them, or even no movement at all.

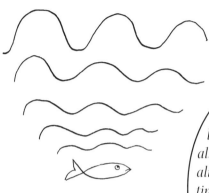

Start by repeating Step 8; and then, when you are ready, think of two people who make you feel angry or hurt. Accept your feelings, even if you don't like them. Ask yourself what is the fear that lies beneath my anger or hurt?

Imagine the person you are angry with in the chair opposite you and just openly tell them how you feel. When you have finished, imagine the light of peace or forgiveness flowing from your heart to theirs.

Now mentally ask yourself what you need to learn from the event, and retain the learning. Allow yourself to release any limiting emotions associated with the event, your heart will store away the wisdom it has given you, either consciously or unconsciously.

You may like to repeat the Starlight meditation on page 26, or do the Sunlight visualization on page 38, after this exercise.

'When you surrender and let go of the past, you allow yourself to be fully alive in the moment. Letting go of the past means that you can enjoy the dream that is happening right now.'
Don Miguel Ruiz

IN MY OWN HEALING JOURNEY, I have realized peace is dependent on patience and self-love. At times I've been consumed with grief and felt rage in my heart. Here, I've found it is important to surrender to my tears and accept the pain, until in emptiness and tiredness I truly seek to let go!

Opposite is an exercise which I hope my help.

SECTION TWO   COURAGE ON THE CATWALK OF LIFE

A SIMPLE EXERCISE, to reconnect to your inherent inner beauty, is to look at a beautiful flower, maybe a rose. At first you see its beauty, its form, yet beyond this form is energy, a stillness, a spaciousness. This is the creative life-force, the divine light that permeates all life.

Behind the rose's beauty, feel, sense and see a gentle light emanating radiance and love within and around the rose.... Now breathe that light into your whole being and sense peace, warmth, security, strength and love filling your whole body with this connective light.

If you have angry, intolerant, jealous, guilty or sad energy stored in your heart shine your own inner love over every atom, every cell of your body to help release this energy.

Consciously move this feeling of love into the heart, the belly, the liver, the stomach and other digestive organs; to the bones, blood, nervous system, to the whole of the body. Imagine all the cells and energy of your body as happy, healthy and harmonious.

Now gently scan your body looking for any blocks in the flow of light. If you find any areas simply pour this abundant universal light onto the area and see it release and transform in the light.

Now imagine this gorgeous golden light spreading out into the energy field around your body. With each inhalation feel more love and light filling your whole body and with each exhalation see this light extending from your aura out further and further.

This beautiful golden light is sealing peace, joy, love, unity and harmony into your whole being and into the energy you share. Remember universal energy is abundant: you can embrace it and even wear it as a cloak of love whenever you feel exhausted by life.

A FOCUS FOR MEDITATION

TAKING A LOOK WITHIN

Stand in front of a mirror. See the light of love in your eyes, your smile and your heart. In this light, begin to accept all the parts of yourself.

Let your mind consider all aspects of yourself: the vulnerable and strong; peaceful and angry; frightened and adventurous; patient and intolerant; joyous and fearful. Just allow yourself to explore your whole emotional experience.

Be kind to yourself. Avoid any criticism, completely allowing yourself to be loving and lovable towards yourself. Do not judge your emotions, accept them. Take care of yourself lovingly and with respect. Close your eyes and give thanks for the light of truth you are experiencing in the current moment.

Now think of one thing which makes you feel really vulnerable. Accept your vulnerability, taking time to love it tenderly.

As a mother might to her child, tell yourself it is okay to be frightened, we all get frightened. Now

get creative. Make this an opportunity to imagine all the wonderful possibilities that lie beyond your fear.

SECTION 3:
INDIVIDUAL
AND
GLOBAL
STYLE

'BE THE CHANGE YOU WANT TO SEE in the world' is the brilliant advice given to us by Mahatma Gandhi. I love this statement, because it powerfully yet simply ignites the senses into action. We are the design team that can create world change through personal and collective consciousness.

Our power lies deep within our hearts, in our shining spirit which has the power to overcome all things. We can choose 'now' to rethink our individual life and the world we live in.

We have looked at the mind and the emotions, so now it is time to tune into our true power—the mystery, joy and love of our true spirituality.

For some crazy reason, people have the idea that being spiritual is to denounce and reject society. You know the old jibe about being 'so heavenly as to be no earthly good'? As a statement of what we need to be, this could not be further from the truth. True spirituality galvanizes us into global citizenship. Rather than denouncing society, we become more involved. We become motivated to live a worthwhile life by taking responsibility for ourselves and for our planet.

Don't confuse your spirituality with religion. Religion can conjure up a whole load of different meanings depending upon whom you ask. Spirituality is simple. It is about 'realizing' our true self, buried deep within our being, where we experience the sacred in all things, including ourselves!

Sometimes our mind and emotions can be ruled by personal gain only. Our spirit, however, resonates with the spirit in all things. Our spirit ignites our senses toward the understanding or recognition of a fabulous flow of energy (or life-force) interpenetrating all life, linking us all to a great universal unseen spiritual reality.

Spiritual practices act as our guide in the deeper journey of understanding who we are and our role in the universe. Within all of us lives a power that is sometimes described as our eternal, higher, spiritual, radiant or shining self. It can also be thought of as our intuition or ageless knowing.

When we connect with our spirit, our awareness moves beyond our immediate family needs to the worldwide needs of humanity. The attributes of the spirit—wisdom, love and power—lead our mind and emotions into poise and calm. They support gentleness and love in our actions, thoughts and speech.

Meditation is in every sense the most 'divine'

way to discover our true self and make way for it. It can't solve all of our problems, but it can help us put our life into perspective. It can also help us directly change our perspective simply and clearly.

Meditation provides the space we require for redesigning our thoughts and feelings, to be congruent with 'who we want to be' and representative of the 'the life we want to live.'

I've never met a person who has not been confused or suffered at some point or other in their life. The power of our spirit uplifts and inspires us to transcend our suffering, and become part of the growing consciousness to cease suffering for all. I believe, without doubt, that our spirit itself contains the powerful humanitarian aid that will release all pain and foster true healing.

The world is full of problems that we can try and help change. We can't just live for today: we have a moral and ethical role in making the world a better place to live in, not only for ourselves, but for our children and their children.... If each of us takes responsibility for our little part of the world, then we really do have a chance of creating beauty in our lives and the lives of future generations.

All that one gives to others one gives to oneself. If this truth is understood, who will not give to others.
Ramana Maharshi

YOUR SACRED SPACE

By now, you may be realizing that at times it makes sense to be quiet and alone to connect with our inner self. You may find the idea of your own meditation, prayer, inner change space very compelling.

Here are some tips for creating and using a special place or sanctuary where you can retreat for renewal, rejuvenation, release and relaxation.

❂ The size of the space doesn't matter—a chair dedicated to peace will do!

❂ Create a small altar where you can place tangible objects to meditate upon—candles, a flower, crystals, images. Ensure whatever you place on your altar inspires you and promotes feelings of love.

❂ Whatever space you have, keep it simple and uncluttered, to promote a clear state of mind.

❂ Just as your body is the temple housing your inner spirit, your sanctuary is a gateway to the glory of your true self. Always try to enter your sanctuary in peace.

❂ Choose a regular time to release your shining spirit and sustain the growth of your true shining self!

THIS SIMPLE PRACTICE promotes the awakening of our spirit. Imagine a beautiful golden sun glowing with golden radiant light. With each inbreath, feel the warmth of the sun's rays; and with each outbreath, sense a relaxing, comforting, golden light flooding your whole being....

Now direct this golden light directly into your heart, feeling your chest expanding as you begin to go deeper and deeper into relaxation. You may begin to feel a warm sense of love and joy filling the very core of your being. Now as you inhale silently, affirm gentleness; and as you exhale silently affirm love. Really begin to associate with the feelings of gentleness and love....

Feel the beautiful sense of serenity that accompanies your own gentleness and love. After a while, you may notice a ray of light from the sun connecting directly with your heart. The radiance of the sun floods your whole being with light. You may begin to feel lighter; you may experience a sense of weightlessness as your spirit is lifted into the heart of the sun. Be aware of the powerful radiance of the sun filling your whole being with divine light.

Now imagine the most beautiful version of yourself before you. See the gentleness and love of your true spirit shining back at you. Feel the unconditional love of your radiant self, accepting every aspect of your nature. There is no harshness or condemnation, only pure gentleness and love. Allow yourself completely to accept this love.

Step into this radiant self you have created. Feel how wonderful it is to see the world through eyes of gentleness and love.

From this new perspective, you can really appreciate yourself and recognize your qualities. You can notice in detail all the wonderful attributes you have. You may even see beautiful, strong and loving qualities in yourself you had not noticed before. Enjoy appreciating yourself for as long as you like! Then gently deepen your breath and once again return your focus to daily living, with a renewed focus of gentleness and love.

> *Fear speaks to you in logic and reason. It assumes the language of love itself. Fear tells you, 'I want to make you safe'. Love says, 'You ARE safe'.*
> Emmanuel

I USED TO GET VERY CONFUSED over the concept of living in spiritual love. I felt overwhelmed by the idea of living in perfection. It just seemed so hopeless: me with all my human frailties! How could I possibly overcome all the pain, fear and doubt I had experienced in my material and physical life?

Then the most gorgeous thing happened. I realized that returning to the pure seed of love in my heart only called for my best. I realized that in the space of eternity there is time to unfold my inner joy and light. I did not have to be perfect today! My key responsibility was to aspire to create with love for myself, others and world we live in.

What I was working toward was the release of fear and the creation of living in love and joy. I still make mistakes sometimes, falling under the spell of fear in one of its many guises, but now I remember I have a choice—I can choose love. What is really beautiful is that with practice this choice becomes the creative power which transforms our life to the new vision of living in harmony and joy.

Our spiritual inner guidance does not force us or hurry us along. It only calls on us to awaken the power of love in our hearts, at our own pace, until the day comes when all our material responses are infused with the wisdom of spiritual love. The power of the spirit, resting in our hearts, leads us towards a path of thankfulness; and it is the true miracle of living.

Even in sadness, we can call upon our inner spiritual power for strength and healing. We can redirect our focus to the power of love within our own hearts. I don't deny this seems tremendously difficult when in the midst of our pain, yet we can ignite the power of our spirit to overcome the conditions in life which fill us with despair.

My Baby is Hurting

When Ben and Dan, our twin sons, were fifteen months old, Ben mysteriously stopped walking. We fled straight to the hospital. After Ben had experienced a series of painful and confusing tests and x-rays, the doctors found lesions in his bone marrow and that his blood count was very low.

When I heard this, I felt as though my heart was trying to punch its way out of my chest. I stammered to the doctor, 'My sister died of the strain of leukaemia most common in children.' It was just awful. We were so helpless, and our beautiful little boy so small, so fragile.

Thankfully, further tests proved Ben's blood to be healthy. After five days, the hospital arranged for us to fly to Liverpool for a CAT scan, to look for a mass on his spine, which could be either malignant or benign. My head was spinning with the sheer horror of it all.

When we got back to Ben's room, Mark and I held each other, as the hot sting of tears washed over my cheeks. We felt dreadful, and I knew I had to centre myself to be strong for Ben, acutely aware that at some level I was sharing fear with my baby. I had to meditate in order to find inner strength. Ben needed it.

I found a quiet space. In an instant, I felt wrapped in beautiful golden radiance. It was as though the windows of my soul had been flung open and the spiritual sunlight of love filled every atom of my being. I then experienced an expanded awareness, realizing my body was part of a greater body: a transforming, powerful energy source. I was aware of my spirit being connected to the spirit in all things. The universal energy of love and healing flooded my whole being.

Then the most amazing thing happened. Our darling Ben's gorgeous smiling face lit up the whole room, bathed in sheer radiance and golden light, and I just knew he would be well. It was like I was experiencing the power of the universe through my own eyes, watching this amazing love completely illuminating Ben.... At the level of my normal consciousness, it was completely awesome; yet at this sacred universal level of consciousness it was as normal and natural as breathing.

Within four days of this experience Ben was walking properly again. We were never given any medical diagnosis for his condition. Did the magnificence of the universe step in or not? I can't prove it did. However, I can say with certainty, that there is a power beyond us that we can access if we try.

WE ALL HAVE GOOD AND BAD FEELINGS. Instead of denying feelings that make us uncomfortable we can accept them as part of us. With self-love, courage, and acceptance, we can transform our feelings to bring balance to our inner world. I find the practice opposite very useful in promoting forgiveness and releasing old pain.

WHO AM I HURTING?

Let yourself relax, and then visualize the face of someone who has hurt you, someone you feel unable to forgive. Take a moment to feel the emotions you are feeling. Now open your eyes and recognize there is only you in the room; they are not here. Now ask yourself 'If I continue not to forgive this person, who am I hurting?' The answer is you!

Whatever the emotional confusion, whether hate or grief, it is a part of you which deserves your love and gentleness. If we can try to accept a crisis as an opportunity to grow, we make room for our own spiritual reconnection.

Usually some form of fear lies beneath anger, such as fear of abandonment or not being good enough. It could be fear of being rejected or misunderstood, or fear of feeling overwhelmed, guilty or depressed. All of these can make us feel separate and disconnected from our strong and shining spirit.

DESIGNING YOUR LIFE begins with your thinking and a self-belief derived from deep inner knowing. Deepak Chopra, M.D., reminds us: 'Everyone has a purpose in life ... a unique gift or special talent to give to others. And when we blend this unique talent with service to others, we experience the ecstasy and exultation of our own spirit, which is the ultimate goal of all goals.' Making the beautiful connection with our inner spirit is a very powerful source of inspiration. Connecting with our spirit goes beyond the commonsense decision to reduce stress and anxiety through meditation; it renews us with greater strength and motivation.

> *Try to be at peace with yourself and help others share that peace. If you contribute to others' happiness, you will find the true goal, the meaning of life.*
> The Dalai Lama

Let yourself become aware of your inner spirit—the powerful urge within your being that is creative, original, imaginative, forward-thinking, responsible and loving. Now let your mind dream of inventive ways in which you can help others and yourself become happier.

Write down ten ways in which you can be more responsible, loving and gentle with yourself, others and with the world. You'll be amazed at how resourceful you can be with a little thought and effort.

Another great way of positively focusing our thoughts is to consider three things (a) that you like about yourself and (b) that make you really unique. Lynne Frank advocates: '*Recognize your gifts and delegate the rest.*'

We are most often our own harshest critics, so it is fundamental that we become more gentle and loving with ourselves. If we look for love and see the beauty in life in the world around us, correspondingly we will see more love in ourselves.

Use thankfulness to help you reconnect to your inner spirit further. For the next week, why not start your day by thinking of five things to be thankful for in your life? Maybe love and kindliness from others; a beautiful home, fantastic husband or wife; gorgeous children; great friends; aspirations; the beauty in nature; your strength; your ability to help others; your faith or your positive outlook....

TAKE A MOMENT TO RELAX and get comfortable. Now reflect on your dreams. Think about some of the things you've always wanted to do. Cast your mind as far back as childhood, and just let yourself remember all the things you have ever dreamed of achieving. Now make a list of your dreams. Go through the list, maybe revising or deleting one or two, and then choose one you could do if you really wanted to.

Whatever you set your heart upon, make sure it fills you with excitement, expectancy and desire: the magnetic ingredients to pull your dreams to you. We gain a greater sense of our 'self' and our 'purpose' when we are pursuing our dreams. It can help us through the most trying and challenging times.

Remember to integrate your passion, your talent, your experience and your love into the creation of your dreams. Do not worry about what talents others have, focus on yours. We are equal, and our dreams can direct us on a journey of unity. As we unfold our inner light, we start to create fabulous ways in which we can serve the world. What do you dream of? When we do what we love, our personal light shines out to the world—maybe unnoticed by others, but uplifting, and literally healing humanity with our joy!

LET'S TAKE A MOMENT TO DREAM.... Close your eyes and visualize yourself on a beautiful beach. Experience the warmth of the sun; feel the sand beneath your feet and the breeze in your hair. Smell the sea salt air and imagine your breath in rhythm with the water as it flows towards you. Notice the perfect blue sky and breath in a vast sense of calmness and oneness with nature as you walk on....

You may have a towel with you. You lie on the golden sand and relax in the warmth of the sun's rays. While you are here, think of your dream and imagine how you will achieve it. Think of some lovely images that sum up your dream. Involve all your senses in the creation of your dream.

Imagine it. What is happening when you have achieved your dream? How do you look? What are you feeling? What are you saying to yourself? Are others congratulating you? Feel yourself smiling with confidence. For instance, to help create a loving relationship ... imagine yourself sharing a romantic dinner, feel the gentle touch of his or her hand, taste the beautiful food, see yourself smiling....

IT IS EASIER THAN YOU THINK TO DO THE RIGHT THINGS TO SAVE OUR PLANET. The organization Friends of the Earth (**http://www.foei.org**) share six key principles:

Buy less stuff.	**Cut your fossil-fuel use.**	**Take out the toxins.**
Choose a local diet.	**Do whatever you can.**	**Spread the word.**

The following list shares some ideas to support those principles.

- Turn off unnecessary lighting and buy energy-saving bulbs.
- Walk, cycle or take public transport wherever possible.
- Recycle your old mobile phones: see **www.fonebak.org** for more info.
- Decline plastic bags whenever possible. A plastic bag can take up 500 years to decay in landfill!*
- Seems obvious: plant a tree....
- Have a bath with someone you love for that extra energy save!
- Turn your thermostat down by one degree. You can save on average £25/$40 a year.*
- Give loose change to charity: 1p or 1c, per person, per week, adds up to £30 million a year in the UK —$150 million in the USA with its larger population!*
- Put gum in the bin: the UK alone spends £150 million p.a. cleaning chewing gum off the streets.*
- Recycle your old spectacles: 200 million people around the world need glasses every year.*
- Recycle old computers: **www.computer-aid.org** can help distribute them to developing countries.
- Buy local produce. Check out **www.farmersmarkets.net**. Maybe start your own vegetable patch.

*The information marked with an asterisk is taken from a wonderful little book I found called CHANGE THE WORLD FOR A FIVER. It inspires people to use their everyday actions to change the world! It is only UK£5, and full of great insights (ISBN 1-904095-96-8). Get it from booksellers or from **http://www.wearewhatwedo.org.**

HELPING THE WORLD BECOME A BETTER PLACE to live in can be easier than you think. Our personal lives are full of responsibilities, and sometimes it is difficult to make time to consider how we can practically help the planet. The list below gives achievable ideas, in everyday areas, where you can enhance the energy systems of the world. I think everyone can make most of the small changes I suggest below:

What stops me getting involved?	**Small changes that collectively can make big differences**
☺ *Going to work*	Donate instead £2/$3 a month to a charity of your choice
☺ *Cleaning the house*	Use eco-friendly natural based products
☺ *Doing the shopping*	Buy more organic and Fair Trade products
☺ *Retail clothes therapy*	Give your old clothes to charity shops
☺ *Mowing the lawn*	Do it once a month. Save water and help the grass self-seed
☺ *Painting the house*	Use water-based paints to cut down on toxic fumes
☺ *Sorting out the mail*	Return all unsolicited junk mail, marking it 'Not known'
☺ *Exercising*	Walk or cycle to your class, reducing fumes and increasing energy
☺ *Preparing meals*	Recycle all packaging. Maybe make compost with leftovers!
☺ *Got to get the children to school*	Start a walking bus group. Cut out fumes and reduce school runs

Ask yourself, 'Which three or four of the above can I do to help in the world today?' What else can I add? Write your ideas down and place them on your fridge as a reminder of your ability to affect world change. Take action today! **Do one thing on your list right away to enhance the path of global togetherness!**

SECTION THREE   INDIVIDUAL AND GLOBAL STYLE

WE ARE ALL LINKED to the great energy-sources of the world through our own inbuilt energy. As our energy-systems interrelate with the world's energy-systems, we can practically alter the outer environment by our actions and attitudes.

The following practice is designed to help us feel oneness with the natural world around us. First, use Step 9 to expand your consciousness and connect with the spirit of love in your own heart.

Imagine you are in a beautiful garden with the most exquisite flowers. Breathe in the essence of the flowers. Become aware of their fragrance, texture, vibrancy and colour. Let yourself fully appreciate their beauty.

Now extend your appreciation to the earth: the soil which nurtures the shrubs, flowers, grass, rocks and trees. Feel the ground beneath you, supporting and sustaining you throughout life. See it all pulsating with the invisible life-force that connects us all. Really become at-one with the magnificence of the earth, and now think of one thing you can do to help preserve this beautiful land....

After a while, you find yourself ascending a path of golden light to the top of a mountain. When you reach the summit, you feel the freshness of the breeze in your hair, as the gentle wind blows. You may now find yourself stretching your arms wide to embrace the purity of the air around you. As a guardian of the earth, imagine how you can help create and sustain purity in the air we breathe...

Now look out at the vast sea. Relaxing, let your breath feel like the rhythm of the sea. Feel the awesomely powerful, cleansing force it can be. Imagine yourself gracefully diving deep into the sea and enjoying a feeling of oneness with the water element. What changes can you make to your lifestyle to reduce water pollution...?

Now allow your spirit to take flight directly into the sun, and feel yourself being energized and renewed in the radiance of the Sun. Before finishing, take this opportunity really to appreciate the nature around you and give thanks for the natural beauty we have inherited in our world.

BEING LOVING AND GENEROUS is a beautiful gift to share with others. Remember that we all have our own unique talent that we bring to the world. The thing we love doing most is the thing we can share with others. It's no good doing something you hate in order to help humanity: it will only fill you with frustration, anger and resentment. It is far more valuable to do something you love to help the world grow.

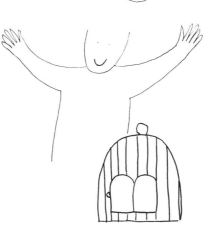

When we enjoy ourselves, everyone around us shares in that enjoyment. Therefore I think it is not only okay to have fun and feel good when supporting the planet, it is essential. As we embrace the spirit of a generous heart, it is good to recognize we can begin with little acts of kindness.

Yes, of course we should all love to act personally and end wars and starvation. Yet it may be more practical to help a local charity or join a group of some kind at first. Being generous and giving really does make us feel happier. We can nourish happiness and love by sowing small seeds of generosity and gratitude in our life through our thoughts, feelings and speech.

Consider one act of kindness you can incorporate into your life, maybe from the list overleaf, which will help make our world a better place to live in.

Mother Teresa shows the way in sharing this thought: 'Don't look for spectacular actions. What is important is the gift of yourselves. It is the degree of love you insert in your deeds.'

'PERHAPS WE'RE TOO EMBARRASSED to change or too frightened of the consequences of showing that we actually care. But why not risk it anyway? BEGIN TODAY! Carry out an act of kindness, with no expectation of reward or punishment. Safe in the knowledge that one day, someone somewhere might do the same for you.' Princess Diana

'Wher-ever you are, whatever your condition is, always try to be a lover.'
Rumi

- Take someone to the shops who doesn't have a car.
- Post a flower to a friend unexpectedly.
- Write small cards of thanks appreciating the people who work for you.
- Give a client your service free occasionally.
- Smile in a traffic jam (more calm energy in the universe!).
- Give a lottery ticket to a stranger (I have not done this one yet!).
- Put little surprises in your partner and/or children's lunch bags.
- Give up your seat on the tube/bus.
- Tell someone they are beautiful, even when they are not feeling down.
- Really listen to someone.
- Stop and ask people if they need help when their car has broken down.
- Make an extra pie/cake for friends with little time.
- Share your time or money to support a good cause.
- See the creative, imaginative genius in everything your children do.
- Be a buddy to someone lonely or in hospital.
- Tell people you love that you love them.
- Help out with neighbours' pets when they are ill or on holiday.
- Compliment a stranger.
- Let people with only a few groceries go before you in the queue.

SECTION 4: PURPOSE-BUILT FOR HAPPINESS!

OUR JOURNEY SO FAR has been leading us to a path of Global Citizenship where social and personal responsibility spring naturally from our inner changes. They are therefore at the forefront of all we do, say and think. We are moving beyond simply knowing that unity between all is the key, to acting upon this knowledge. we are now taking responsibility for ourselves, each other and the world we live in.

We are co-creators, and in many of us momentum is gathering little by little for conscious living. Our collective awakening includes a recognition that living a worthwhile life is less about who we are and more about what we do. Embracing the connective flow of our spirit awakens in our hearts a sense that we are all links in the great chain of evolution—and can create world unity, no matter how slowly, heart to heart, person to person and nation to nation.

We know by this point that making a difference in our individual lives makes a difference to how things play out in the world at large. Our individual actions can create a global purpose of 'working together for peace, for love, for a beautiful new world —in all we think, say and do'.

This fourth section helps us focus on our spirit to co-create a new world in fresh, insightful, inspiring, imaginative and resourceful ways. It develops further our beautiful opportunity to connect to our spirit, calling us to have a deep faith in the reality that we are not only human but also divine.

Amid the disappointments, deceit, suffering, murder, betrayal and wars we have all witnessed, it is the power of spirit that leads us toward love and growth in the most dreadful circumstances, as individuals over many centuries have proved. Faith in true love accelerates our spiritual growth—helping us to transcend our mind and emotions and connect with our eternal knowing.

Our responsibility to embrace world togetherness, kindness and love, magically, is our greatest path to self-love and personal liberation. When we seek to connect to universal love, the most amazing and beautiful thing happens: we find natural and abundant love within ourselves.

WE ARE CHARGED with the delightful opportunity of reprogramming collective consciousness so that it moves along the evolutionary path from fear to love. This is truly exciting. We are in a position individually to raise the consciousness of the world. The only power we are required to have is that of controlling our thoughts for the outcome of good. Then miracles can and will happen.

It is easy for us to see the instant results of our peacemaking on an individual level, which gives us confidence in the biblical maxim that we reap as we sow. On a global level, we are required to demonstrate a greater faith: that the action of our loving kindness today will manifest greater peace, joy and beauty in our world tomorrow.

We all know that love brings us joy—and with joy we feel abundance. Fear, of course, does not disappear: it is still an option. What changes is our choice. We choose to give our attention to love and become part of positive world change.

> *Send out love and harmony, put your mind and body in a peaceful place, and then allow the universe to work in that perfect way that it knows how.*
> Dr Wayne W. Dyer

OVER THE YEARS, TO PULL MYSELF OUT OF PAIN, I have developed a lovely little practice that helps me so much. I hope you enjoy it. It brings a wonderful sense of freedom. Imagine you have no limitations; all your worries, fears and doubts have disappeared. You don't feel confusion, anxiety or depression. You are free from guilt, shame, regret, pain or despair.

In fact, you have growing confidence. You feel happy, courageous, joyous and strong. You have an open heart, filled with compassion and love. You are a very beautiful person: considerate, honest, loving and open. Imagine this world for a moment. Breathe in the sense of lightheartedness that it brings, and truly start to connect with the emotions of delight, happiness and joy. Do this for five minutes or so.

From this perspective take a piece of paper and write at the top of it 'HOW DO I PROMOTE WORLD UNITY?' To help with this step consider the following ideas as you write down your answer.

From now on, let every action, every reaction, every thought, and every emotion be based on love. Increase your self-love until the entire dream of your life is transformed from fear and drama to love and joy.
Don Miguel Ruiz

MY QUESTIONS TO ANSWER

☻ How do I demonstrate I am aware of my role in world (for example, through my words, thoughts, actions)?

☻ How do I take responsibility for our planet?

☻ How do I share responsibility for suffering (e.g. by personal support, charity, advocacy or prayer)?

☻ How do I celebrate diversity, valuing traditions, rituals and core beliefs?

☻ How do I contribute to the community?

☻ How do I care for and love myself?

☻ How do I motivate others and myself to support global togetherness?

☻ How do I create a sense of oneness with all sentient life—people, plants, animals, minerals?

IT IS AS THOUGH WE ARE ALL AWAKENING from a drowsy sleep to find our sense of powerlessness and fear is being cleansed with a fresh life-force of hope and personal responsibility. We are looking beyond the stress and chaos of modern living to the natural beauty of the world.

We can trust in the fact we have the canvas of beauty to work from. It is only our human decisions that can exhaust and strip nature and people of their beauty and freedom. Choosing to focus on the natural bounty and beauty of the earth promotes happiness and security in our hearts, in a human experience where fear could so easily be the choice.

'Hate never dispelled hate. Only love dispels hate. This is the law, ancient and inexhaustible.'
Buddha

Collectively, as we unite around the world to share our voice, the leaders of nations will in the end have no choice but to listen. The mass movements which force governments to act are becoming more and more part of the way of life of people all over the world. We know it is not acceptable that over 30,000 children die daily from poverty in our global society. The wrongness of conditions such as this propels us forward, to make our world a better place to live in for all of us: as can be seen in the pioneering 'Make Poverty History' campaign.

The more we focus on love, the more we see that our choice of love and joy, however simple, must be consistent—as its opposite number, fear, is ever waiting to take its place. Whenever we feel anxiety or a lack of hope, simply choosing to focus on love can realign our thoughts to harmony and unity.

Think of one thing in the world at the moment that really infuriates you and maybe fills you with hatred for the perpetrators. Now ask yourself 'how can I change my response?' Not of course so as to give in, but so as to

❂   create a more loving energy of compassion around this condition

❂   help create physical change in this area with my time, talent or money.

Amid all the tragedy and suffering we experience in our world, we are also seeing massive global togetherness. People from all nations are pulling together in one spirit—as was seen in the generosity of the world after the Boxing Day Tsunami in 2004.

TO HELP ME BREAK DOWN BARRIERS and develop a sense of community, I looked at the various aspects of our outer life. I asked myself, 'how do I share in community life in a supportive way?' I then looked at small achievable steps to which I could commit myself in order to generate a sense of community in my life.

It is our greatest opportunity to spread a sense of shared humanity from person to person. This may involve taking our courage in both hands, and maybe spreading our wings too, beyond what we previously thought we could do. If we have always wanted to be involved in community work but have been to shy to take part, it is now important to pick up our courage and just do it.

The ideas in the next column are some of the things I do to help generate a sense of community in my own life. Several of them, you doubtless do too. Why not give one or two you don't already do a try?

There is nothing to fear except fear.... Resign all to the wisdom and the love embodied in divine law. Do your best. Be true and sincere and loving in your human relationships. Let love rule your heart and your life.
White
Eagle

GLOBAL CITIZENSHIP, LOCAL LEVEL

✪ Introduce yourself to neighbours you see regularly but haven't spoken to

✪ Take the opportunity to welcome new neighbours into the area

✪ Support local endeavours e.g. fêtes, petitions you believe in, or community gatherings

✪ Find out the name of your postal delivery person, refuse or recycling collectors, organic vegetable or milk roundspeople, and greet them where possible.

✪ Find a local church, community centre or charity you can support the work of within your area

✪ Get to know what is going on in local government affecting your area

✪ Be aware of elderly or ill neighbours who may suddenly need your support.

✪ Be consciously grateful for the help and support your community gives you.

SECTION FOUR   **PURPOSE-BUILT FOR HAPPINESS**

When the Heart Speaks—Listen

I believe the light in our heart is our own individual part of God. When we listen to our hearts, we need not worry whether we should go to right or left, for we feel a sense of certainty that guides us on our way.

Around nine years ago I was invited to volunteer at the White Eagle Lodge in America for three months, based on an offer I had made six months earlier—which had been to volunteer in Canada for three weeks! This invitation came just at the time I needed it. The challenge to quit my job and 'up sticks' was a great turning point in my life and transformed me. I knew little of the Lodge's work, having only read one book of its philosophy, yet I wasn't anxious, it just felt so right. As soon as I turned to my inner guidance, I knew with the deepest faith that the only decision ... was to go.

Blind faith carried me on my journey, blessed with the companion of peaceful inner knowing at my side. Transcending beliefs and experiencing inner knowing can be the most liberating of spiritual gifts. All my friends thought I was mad, and the very physical part of me was inclined to agree. But I wasn't listening to my head, I was following my heart. For me, the heart is our inner sanctuary—where all is attainable and nothing is desired, save a deep love of natural order, as we share in the illumination of God.

A quite different example of miraculous manifestation in my life was when the boys where first born. Moving to the Isle of Man, we had cut down our income by two-thirds, increased our mortgage and become four in one year! Finances were particularly tight and I began to pray for a solution. Loving ceremony, I set up a little ritual of lighting three candles—representing Love, Wisdom and Power—before invoking the great angels of prosperity and abundance to help us.

For three weeks, I visualized beautiful angels pouring golden coins into our house, trusting that the law of magnetic attraction would set in place the conditions for Mark and I to ease the financial pressure on us. Then one day, out of the blue, two people knocked at our door asking could they use our house as a film location for £800 a day! Such is the magic of our universe!

I believe the universe is abundant, and I think this belief makes way for miracles in my life. Time and time again, I have found where my motive is inspired by love, does not adversely affect anyone else or is in service to others, then miracles can and do occur!

YOU MAY LIKE TO START this step by repeating the Starlight or Sunlight meditation. Now become aware of the room and the building you are in … before directing your loving peaceful awareness out into the street. Be aware of your favourite places near your home, gently shining the light of love and peace as you watch…. Now go back into your house, see yourself walking through it, filling it with radiance, love and peace.

Do the same for all areas of your life. See your place of work filled with this gentle, tender beautiful light. Then see your friends and family's houses and schools filled with brilliant glowing light and the social venues you attend filled with the same radiant light.

You may notice a particular part of your life where you are experiencing conflict with another. See that area now … and fill the person or persons involved with wonderful radiant peace. As you continue to breathe in the wonderful energy of loving peace, you feel yourself filled with such great love.

. Now visualize love and peace flowing from your

> *Love is the key to all knowledge, wisdom and power. Dwell deep in this love, and you will see as God sees.*
> CHRIST IN YOU

heart to the town you live in. Extend your loving energy to the state or country you live in. Finally, see the world enveloped in loving light. Imagine the power of peace, promoting love, unity, tenderness, strength and compassion in the world. Now direct that peace, which rides upon the wings of love, to a personal situation of your choice, where it can promote health and happiness….

When you are ready, gently return your awareness to the room, to the chair you are sitting on and the steady rhythm of your breathing.

To help sustain your peace consciousness, continue to focus on peace throughout the day. Feel this peace inspiring the things you say, do and think. Let the essence of your meditation guide your day, extending peace toward yourself and everyone you meet.

As the author Marianne Williamson says, 'Your greatest opportunity to positively affect another person's life is to accept God's love into your own. By being the light you shine the light on everyone and everything.'

TAKE A SHEET OF PAPER and write on it the following statement: 'We are all connected through the spirit of love, no barriers of ethnic origin, gender, religion, age, job status, education, sexual orientation or social position can change the fact we are all equal.'

Now ask yourself, 'Is this statement true for me?' If not, drill down to why it is not. Look at how you have cultivated your beliefs in this area or that area. Are they still true for you? Consciously committing to our own personal, emotional and spiritual growth takes courage. It calls us to evaluate and redefine our core beliefs.

Core beliefs represent our view of the world and are the driving force behind the life we are living. A willingness to accept the power of our thinking is the first step towards consciously creating the life you want to live. As Henry Ford said, 'Whether you think you can or think you can't, you're right!'.

Everything we think and feel reflects who we are. As we have observed, often our responses are echoes of past fears. We can often feel resistance, when reprogramming our thinking, which is quite natural. Don't worry about this, simply use the previous steps to break down old, limiting thoughts and emotions that do not support the sparkling present and future you which to create.

We are on a journey of continuous improvement in how we recreate ourselves. This journey calls us to accept that although we are all different, our individual differences can enrich our life-experience and create a diverse and beautiful world.

Our job is to cut through the mental and emotional chaos created by individual personalities and choose loving kindness in a world where fear could so easily be the choice.

CREATIVE VISUALIZATION is a wonderful technique. It helps us create whatever we deeply want in our life. Whether it is releasing negative thought-patterns or developing our confidence, it can add power to the goals we wish to achieve.

Combining creative visualization and affirmations is a great way to support a change in old core beliefs and to en-

'This world is but a canvas to our imaginations. Dreams are the touchstones of our characters.'
Henry David Thoreau

hance feelings of security, happiness, strength, calm and love in our inner world.

Both techniques involve using our mind, emotions and spiritual power to create what we really want in our life. Essentially, they support our goal and help us imagine and create the self-improvement we desire to manifest. Try this exercise to fine-tune your creativity!

WORKING WITH AFFIRMATIONS

1. Relax deeply, really connecting to your inner spirit. Let your higher conscience support you by listening to your inner wisdom and letting it help you create new positive changes in your life.

2. Now think of something you'd badly like to have, or work towards, something which is an achievable improvement. For example, a new job, a new home, improved physical health, the ability to speak confidently in meetings or when making a difficult phone call, or when you join a new club or apply to a voluntary body.

3. Now let yourself daydream. Get a clear picture or sense of the object or situation you want to create. Think of it as happening now.

4. Focus on it regularly. The more often you think of it, in detail, the easier it will become to project as a reality.

5. Use an affirmation to reinforce your self-improvement. For example, if you want to improve your interviewing skills you might picture yourself handling an interview effortlessly. An affirmation to support this could be 'I am calm, confident and sincere in interviews'.

STEP 37: BECOME EVERYTHING YOU WERE INTENDED TO BE

I THINK WE ALL have a beautiful inner light placed in our heart, which reflects our own personal and powerful gift we bring to the world. Each step we take to unfold that inner light in our life brings us closer to our wonderful purpose in living!

Often, we hold back or feel shy about our talents when in fact our challenge is to be totally comfortable with them. They are part of our physical and spiritual make up. As we listen to our heart, our true feelings may well tell us things we did not want to hear! It is important not to ignore our feelings; they are our guide to finding happiness and self-love in life.

How we progress is really up to us when unfolding our destiny. Our intuition may call for the courage to make huge changes in our lives, like ending relationships, changing our career or moving away from our friends and family.

Sometimes we have to leave behind all that is familiar in order to embrace our own personal destiny—which can be tremendously hard. However, these changes may enhance our world, opening up opportunities for beautiful growth that our intuition knows awaits us!

Contemplate this wonderful quotation from Marianne Williamson's A RETURN TO LOVE.

'Our deepest fear is not that we are inadequate, Our deepest fear is that we are powerful beyond measure. It is our light, not our darkness, that most frightens us.

'We ask ourselves: 'Who am I to be brilliant, gorgeous, talented, fabulous? Actually who are you not to be?

'You are a child of God. Your playing small doesn't serve the world. There is nothing enlightening about shrinking so that other people around you won't feel insecure. We are all meant to shine as children do.'

How true! Now ask yourself 'Do I underplay or overplay my achievements? I am guessing that like me, you are aware of your failings; but do you ever truly embrace and enjoy the success, talent and love you experience and have to offer the world?

Take a moment, let yourself relax and become aware of your talents and gifts. Now ask yourself: a) Do I hide my gifts and talents? b) If I do, what changes can I make to accept all the ways my own beautiful inner light shines?

SECTION FOUR   **PURPOSE-BUILT FOR HAPPINESS**

WE ARE CONSTANTLY GROWING and changing. I have found I have to regularly review my design plans. Use the following ideas and objectives to support continuous improvement in your life and your contribution to the world.

PERSONAL PERFORMANCE ACTION LIST

⚙ **How can I manifest the life I was born to live?** Clearly define your philosophy for achieving your life purpose by creating a personal statement. Include spiritual, emotional and mental attributes.

⚙ **How are you developing your personal vision?** Who can help you and who can you help to create your ideal life? Consider all areas of your life, physical, social, family, work, community and intimate relationships.

⚙ **List three personal goals for the next year.** Include your target date for achieving them and a performance measure to know you have achieved them. Use affirmations and creative visualization and loving determination to create your dreams.

⚙ Use affirmations, creative visualization and loving determination to create your dreams.

⚙ We spend at least forty per cent of our waking life working, so it is important we find our job rewarding. Define the unique talents and services you can offer. If you don't love what you are doing you are not giving your most beautiful God-given talents to the world. **Make small steps to transform your career to the one of your dreams.**

⚙ **Create a personal training and development plan.** Include areas where you can build on your strengths; identify areas where you can develop to support your personal vision; build in any potential costs to finance the creation of your dreams.

In short, continually get to know yourself and what will make your life more worthwhile. Make yourself adaptable by removing barriers and creating advances to generate the life you want to live. Confucius advises each of us 'The essence of knowledge is, having it, to use it.'

THIS MEDITATION helps us sense the wider spectrum of divinity by connecting with the universal spirit made up of the spirit in all life. Billy Graham shares 'individual guardian, guiding angels attend at least some of our ways and hover protectively over our lives'.

Gently allow your breath to become a little deeper. Sense a gentle loving calm caressing your whole being with peace. Fill your inhalation with love, and on each exhalation let your whole body feel a greater sense of love. Imagine the light of a candle, see the exquisite flame glowing out toward your heart. As you connect to the light your whole being is flooded with radiance and love.

Let the flame become a flame of purity and truth that guides you deeper into the heart of your being. The flame can help us remember our true spirit; it can awaken our hearts to the light of truth.

With your inner vision, now become aware of a glorious host of angelic beings, pouring divine love into every atom of your being.

Let yourself feel their companionship and support, let their light guide you further into truth. Great love and beauty fills every cell of your being now. Let this light flood your whole being. As you do so, you will be awakening the universal spirit of love in your own heart.

Now envisage that you are an angel; a complete body of light, and you have chosen the physical form to express universal loving light. In this light, even with all of the calamities of the world around us we know we are not helpless. We know we can extend the hand of love to make a positive impact on the world no matter how seemingly small.

Now imagine yourself joining with others all round the world, working together for peace, for freedom and happiness. Feel a lovely sense of unity and togetherness. See beautiful little seed thoughts of light projecting loving energy all over the world. Enjoy this sense of unity and oneness with all life.

> 'God has given you a spirit with wings on which to soar into the spacious firmament of Love and Freedom.'
> Kahlil Gibran

THE FOLLOWING LIST is of actions I have found successful for living in my own life. I think they provide great little reminders for increasing love in our life, the life of others and the world we live in.

- Don't delay in creating a better world. Start today.
- Remember, you are marvellous!
- Create with love in all you say, think and do.
- Do listen—both to your heart and to others.
- Get to know like-minded people and grow a sense of community.
- Celebrate your successes.
- Try to move beyond your pain.
- Have courage. Your courage will not only transform your life, it will transform the world we live in. Don't give up.
- Stop the world so you can meditate daily.
- Be a responsible member of the planet. Care for and respect the environment, others and yourself.
- Be loving. Expect the best and automatically your presence will lift others.
- Treat others the way you would like to be treated. Be ethical and kind.
- Most of all: laugh and really enjoy the life you are living!

Add your own ideas to this list. Then, why not blow up your blueprints for living to poster size and place it somewhere prominent in your home or work, as a daily reminder of your commitment to being loving in all you think, say and do?

CONCLUSION

OUR WORLD IS GOOD HANDS—our hands. We all have the power to make a difference in life, working together to for peace, healing and happiness. Together we are learning to live dynamically, respecting and loving each other—ourselves, and the planet we live in.

I firmly believe that when we connect to our spiritual essence of love, joy and abundance we shall usher in a better way of living. Without doubt, the cumulative effect of our thoughts, words and actions will create a beautiful new world.

For now, our individual challenge is to ensure creating from gentleness and love is a personal reality for us. Don't be put off by that. Do what you can: all our individual small improvements add to the quality of universal consciousness.

What is truly lovely is that within us all rests the Source of true healing, and that together, little by little, person to person, and community to community we can and will affect world change and awaken global togetherness in our hearts and the heart of the world.

Consciousness creates reality. We are now collectively asking 'How can I change it? How can I make it better?' How can I make it more beautiful?'. It is our choice and delight to join with the creative force of the Universe.

This won't always be easy: it takes sheer determination, guts and self-love to achieve. Yet it brings the most astonishing rewards, principally the inner knowing that 'within each of us is enough courage and love to unfold a more loving life and a better world to live in.'

The amazing thing about choosing to stop our suffering is that it naturally leads to a second choice of 'becoming part of the growing evolution to cease all suffering'. Inner personal peace is truly connected to world peace. What is very inspiring is that it is we ourselves who have the power to make the world a better place to live in.

With this in mind, our greatest task is to eliminate the war in our own hearts, which is a beautiful step on the road to peace and love. What is that road, the road to peace and love? Well, it simply is the one on which we stop choosing to nurture personal irritation, pain, fear, denial, anger and judgment, and live by the light of our own love.

The call is to shift our focus to self-love and self-healing—and that also increases the energy of love we draw from, collectively. Our task is not to change others, it is to change ourselves, so that the 'flame' of peace and love burning in our hearts touches the hearts of those we meet. Remember: '**Our personal change can affect the transformation of the world.**'